I'M A FUTURE ENGINEER!

Written By Manisha Nayak
Illustrated By Eliz Ong

WS Education

NEW JERSEY • LONDON • SINGAPORE • BEIJING • SHANGHAI • TAIPEI • CHENNAI

Published by
WS Education Pte. Ltd.
5 Toh Tuck Link, Singapore 596224

National Library Board, Singapore Cataloguing in Publication Data
Name(s): Nayak, Manisha. | Ong, Eliz, illustrator.
Title: I'm a future engineer! / written by Manisha Nayak ; illustrated by Eliz Ong.
Other Title(s): I'm a future scientist!
Description: Singapore : WS Education, [2026]
Identifier(s): ISBN 978-981-98-1030-7 (hardcover) | 978-981-98-1031-4 (paperback) | 978-981-98-1032-1 (book for institutions) | 978-981-98-1033-8 (book for individuals)
Subject(s): LCSH: Engineering--Juvenile literature. | Engineers--Juvenile literature. | Engineering--Vocational guidance--Juvenile literature.
Classification: DDC 620--dc23

British Library Cataloguing-in-Publication Data
A catalogue record for this book is available from the British Library.

Desk Editor: Daniele Lee

Printed in Singapore

CONTENTS

Say 'Hello' to Rob!

Have you ever looked at something fascinating and wanted to take it apart to see how it works? Are you curious about things and excited about solving problems? Well, you may just have the makings of an engineer in you!

Engineers are people who design and build products, machines and structures. From toys to computers to bridges to spacecraft, engineering can be found everywhere. Engineers apply their knowledge of mathematics and science for the benefit of mankind.

Fancy a career as an engineer when you grow up? Read on and get to know all about the exciting world of engineering!

All the best! Robo

It Takes All Kinds!

Engineering is a broad field. It is divided into several branches. Engineers in different branches do very different things. However, engineers from different branches often need to work together to create complex systems.

I plan, design and supervise the construction and maintenance of structures such as buildings, bridges and roadways.

Civil engineer

I use advances in technology and medicine to develop new devices and equipment that improve human health.

Biomedical engineer

I design, develop, test and implement computer software and hardware systems.

I design, develop and test aircraft, spacecraft and missiles.

Electrical engineer

I design, develop, test and manage the manufacturing of electrical equipment used in various systems.

I design, develop and test machinery, equipment and technology to help improve a farm's efficiency.

Agricultural engineer

I design, build and maintain marine vessels such as ships, boats and submarines.
Marine engineer

I develop and design manufacturing processes to transform materials into products such as detergents and paper.
Chemical engineer

I develop, process and test materials used to create various products such as sporting gear and aeroplane wings.

I design, develop, test and implement robotic systems for various purposes.

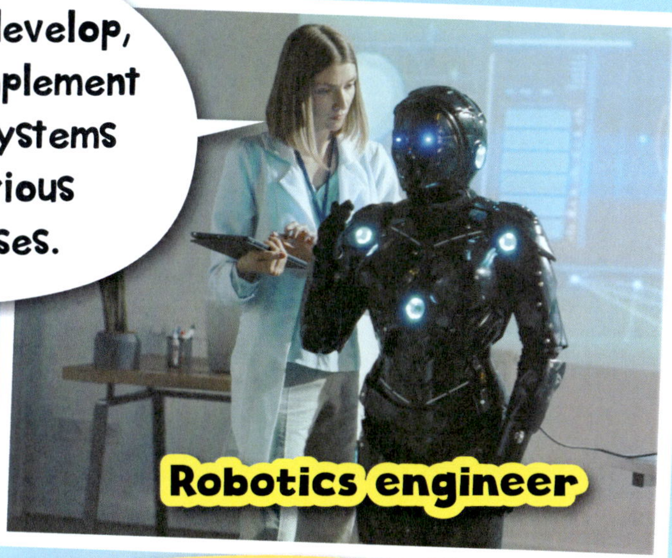

Other than these, there are many more branches of engineering. Which one excites you the most?

Did You Know?

The term 'engineering' is said to be derived from the Latin word '*ingenium*', which means 'cleverness'. Let's find out some more fun facts about engineering!

Standing at a staggering height of 828 metres, the Burj Khalifa in Dubai is the world's tallest building. More than 300 engineers were involved in its construction!

The world's first general-purpose computer, ENIAC, was created in 1945. It weighed as much as several elephants!

Engineers from many fields have worked together to make a type of brick using mushrooms! These bricks are strong, and naturally resistant to water, mould and fire. And of course, they're environmentally-friendly too!

Everyday Engineering

If you thought engineering was a field of study that involves only gigantic structures or complex machinery, think again! Engineering is actually present behind the simplest of things we use in our everyday lives!

Look around your home. The pen you write with, your watch that tells you the time, the light bulb that brightens your room, the mattress you sleep on, engineering was used to make almost everything!

Most of the things you see around you are the products of many engineers from different fields putting their brains together. For example, an electric toothbrush has a team of materials engineers, chemical engineers, mechanical engineers, electrical engineers and others behind it!

Which is the most impressive engineering marvel in your room?

Upwards and Onwards

The work of an engineer is never done. Even after building something, engineers are constantly striving to improve it. Thanks to this progressive mindset, we have countless technological advancements that enrich our everyday lives!

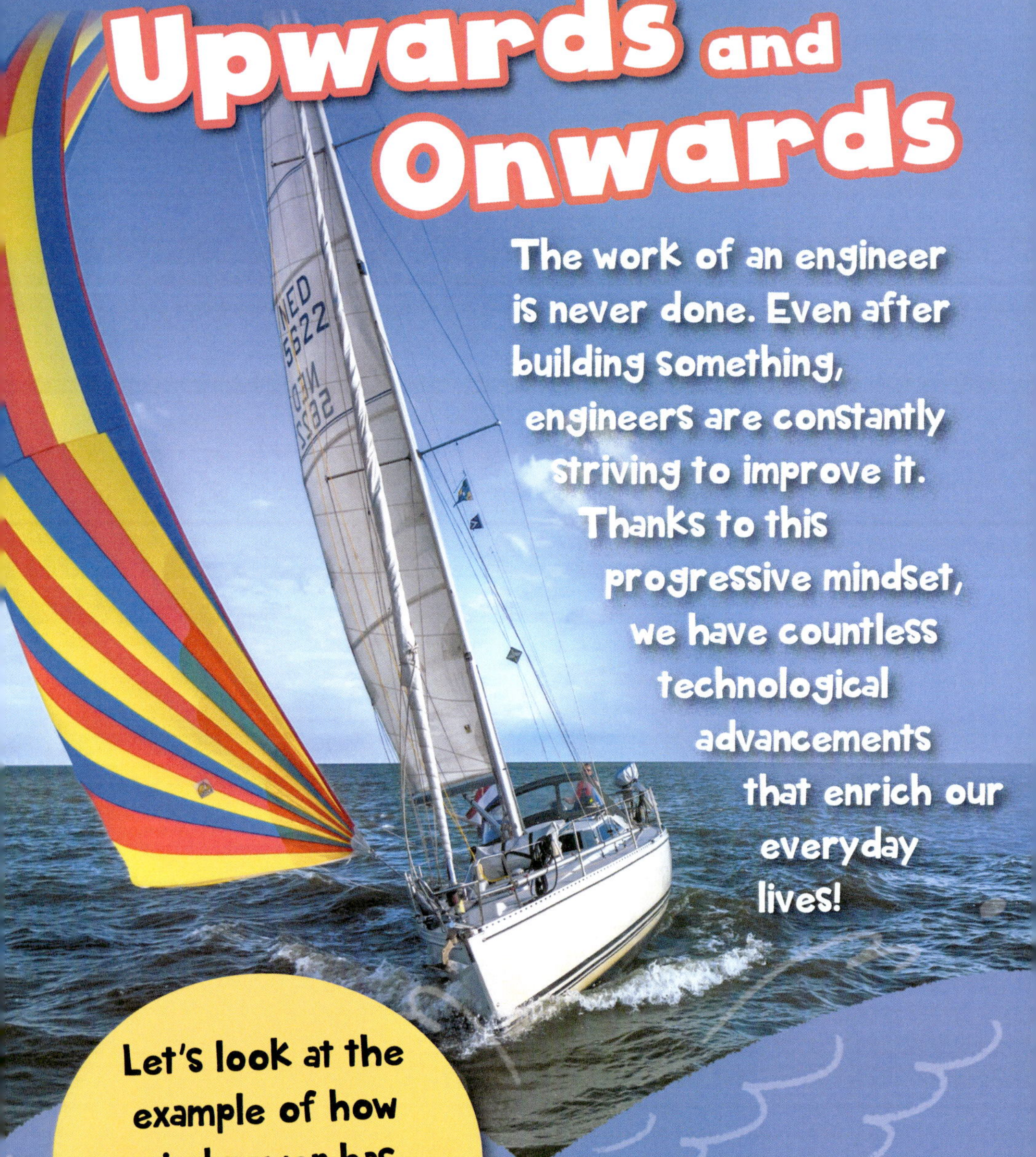

Sailors have been using wind to propel their boats and ships for thousands of years.

Over time, simple windmills were built to make use of the power of wind to grind grains and pump water.

In 1887, a Scottish electrical engineer called James Blyth built the first known wind turbine. He used it to power the lighting in his cottage, making it the first house in the world to have wind-powered electricity.

Over the years, advances in technology allowed humans to harness wind as a renewable source of energy. Today, wind turbines are commonly used in many parts of the world to generate electricity.

Let's Make a Windmill!

What you need

- A square piece of paper
- A pair of scissors
- A push pin
- Glue
- A straw

What you need to do

1. Fold the piece of paper diagonally twice to find its centre.

2. Cut along the folded lines but do not cut all the way till the centre.

3. Bend each cut end and glue it to the centre to make the windmill.

4. Attach the windmill to the straw using a push pin.

5. Blow at the windmill or position it near a fan to watch it spin!

Ancient Marvels

Engineering is not a new field. It has existed since ancient times. Thousands of years ago, humans made and used simple machines, such as the wheel, to make their work easier.

With time, the products and structures they made became more and more complex. Even today, scientists are baffled over how exactly some of the structures from thousands of years ago were built without modern engineering equipment and methods.

The pyramids of Giza

The famous pyramids of Giza in Egypt were built about 4500 years ago. The largest of them, known as the Great Pyramid, was built to a staggering height of 147 metres using 2.3 million blocks of stone, each weighing about 2,500 kilograms!

The Great Wall of China

One of the most recognised structures in the world, the Great Wall of China is a marvel of engineering and construction.

The wall, spanning more than 20,000 kilometres, was built by China's emperors to protect their territory. Construction, carried out under multiple dynasties, lasted more than 2000 years!

Isn't it mind-boggling that such a massive and complex structure was built without the construction equipment of today?

The Taj Mahal

The ivory-white marble Taj Mahal, situated in India, is well recognised all over the world. It was commissioned by Mughal emperor Shah Jahan in memory of his wife Mumtaz Mahal.

The Taj Mahal was built over 17 years by about 22,000 workers. It is widely admired for its perfect symmetry and intricate art.

Millions of tourists visit the Taj Mahal every year.

The Engineering Design Process

Engineers need to do a lot of problem-solving at work. They usually follow a series of steps to come up with solutions to the problem. This is known as the engineering design process.

There are several steps in the engineering design process. There are also variations of the process, depending on the problem the engineers are trying to solve.

Ask — Define the problem.

Imagine — Brainstorm to generate ideas.

Plan — Select a solution.

Create — Make the item.

Test — Evaluate the item.

Improve — Make the item better.

Share — Present the results.

How would you use the engineering design process to solve an everyday problem you face?

Inspired by Nature

Nature has always fascinated humans. Did you know that engineers often look towards nature for inspiration to build new things? Let's look at a few examples!

Shinkansen trains

Shinkansen trains in Japan are known for their high speeds. They can travel at speeds of more than 300 kilometres per hour!

However, when the trains were first designed, they were very noisy. Engineers needed a way to reduce the noise without making the trains slower.

One of the engineers, Eiji Nakatsu, was an avid bird-watcher. He had observed that kingfishers could dive smoothly into the water to catch fish, hardly creating a splash.

Drawing inspiration from the kingfisher, the front of the train was redesigned to mimic a kingfisher's beak. Shinkansen trains with this new design became faster, quieter and also used less electricity!

Velcro fasteners

Velcro fasteners are commonly found in shoes, clothing and bags. Did you know that their invention was inspired by nature?

Swiss engineer George de Mestral was out for a walk with his dog when he noticed that seeds of the burdock plant had stuck to his socks and his dog's fur. Close observation showed that the seeds had tiny hooks that had fastened to the fabric of his socks and his dog's fur.

Inspired by the burdock seeds, de Mestral invented Velcro, a fastener consisting of hooks on one strip that could attach to loops on another strip. These fasteners are now common all over the world! Can you find an example of them in your home?

Detective Work

Take a close look at these pictures of famous structures around the world. Can you identify these feats of engineering and their locations correctly?

a

b

c

d

e

f

g

h

Find the answers on page 55!

Out of the World!

One of humanity's greatest engineering feats is something that is out of the world. Quite literally so!

The International Space Station (ISS) is a large spacecraft orbiting the Earth about 400 kilometres above it. Operated jointly by five space agencies from 15 countries, the ISS serves as a living and working space for astronauts from all over the world.

The ISS orbits the Earth once in about 90 minutes.

Did you know that the ISS is larger than a six-bedroom house? End to end, it is 109 metres long and weighs more than 400,000 kilograms!

View of the Earth from a circular window (known as a porthole) in the ISS

Astronauts live in the ISS for months, studying space and carrying out experiments. They also go outside the ISS for spacewalks.

An astronaut on a spacewalk

Hundreds of astronauts have been to the ISS since it was built. Astronauts typically spend about six months in the ISS before they come back to the Earth.

WORD WHIZ

spacewalk: any activity done by an astronaut in space outside a spacecraft

Building and maintaining this extremely complex system would not be possible without the best engineering brains from multiple countries coming together.

The ISS has helped scientists to learn a lot about living and working in space!

WORD WHIZ

collaborative: two or more people or groups working together for a particular purpose

A Wobbly Problem

Oh, that's easily fixed! I'll just place a folded piece of paper under that leg.
Good idea!

Oh dear...
What happened?
Now this leg is higher than the others, so the chair is still wobbly.

I think the folded piece of paper is too thick. Let's try folding it fewer times.
Oh yes, that should work.
Yes, this feels just right.

This was fun, thinking of creative ways to solve the problem of my wobbly chair!
YOUNG ENGINEER
Yes! We're like the young engineers in this book, solving problems! I think I may want to become an engineer when I grow up!
Me too! And I think we're *engi-nearly* there!

One week later...
Olive, why are you back under the chair??
The folded piece of paper keeps sliding out from under the leg!
Hmm... We need to put our engineering brains to work again. We can't give up!
TAP! TAP!

I have an idea! Should we stick the folded piece of paper under the chair with glue?
Oh yes, then it will stop sliding out!
GLUE
Great! I think we have solved the problem.

Two weeks later...
Back under the chair again, Olive?
Yes, the chair is wobbly again!
Grrr...
BEFORE
AFTER
I think the folded piece of paper has compressed and become thinner over time under your and the chair's weight. This is causing the chair to wobble again.

We should use a hard and strong material, instead of the folded piece of paper.
Ooh! How about a piece of wood?
Great idea! But where can we get that?
My friend Jane is learning carpentry. I'm sure I can ask her to make a perfectly sized wooden block for me.

GLUE
All right, I got the block from Jane. Let's stick it under the leg using this strong glue!
Perfect! We have finally solved the problem of the wobbly chair.
Yay! Three 'chairs' for our engineering brains!

The end

Mission to

Can humans live on Mars one day? This question has intrigued scientists and engineers for a long time.

Mars has some similarities with the Earth. Both are rocky planets that are believed to have been formed at the same time. The length of a day on Mars is similar to that of a day on the Earth.

Mars!

Mars also has water, though most of it is trapped in ice. Studies have shown that life may have possibly existed on Mars at some point in the past. This makes it very exciting for humans to consider exploring Mars.

However, there are several challenges to overcome before we can pack up and move to Mars.

For example, humans on Mars will need oxygen to breathe and stay alive. The atmosphere on Mars consists mainly of carbon dioxide. Oxygen makes up less than 1% of the air on Mars.

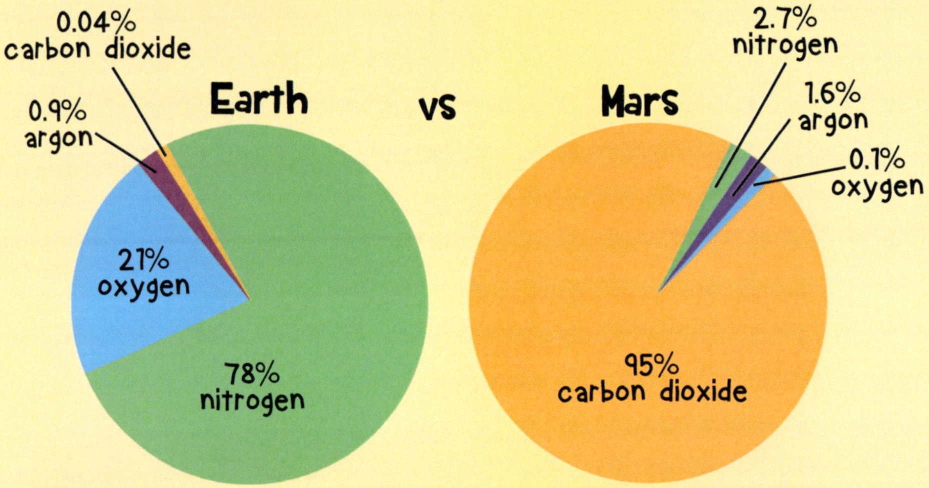

Main gases that make up the air on Earth and Mars

Scientists and engineers are working tirelessly to come up with solutions to these possible challenges.

In July 2020, a rover called Perseverance was launched by NASA to study the environment on Mars, test out new technologies and look for past and present evidence of life.

Perseverance landed on Mars in February 2021. It is hoped that the findings of Perseverance will pave the way for successful human missions to Mars.

WORD WHIZ

NASA: National Aeronautics and Space Administration, a United States government agency responsible for science and technology related to air and space

A device aboard Perseverance was able to extract a small amount of oxygen from the atmosphere of Mars. With technological advances, it may be possible to extract enough oxygen to supply breathable air for humans on Mars in the future.

Can science and engineering help make the red Only time will tell.

I'm Inspired

Leonardo da Vinci is regarded as one of the greatest artists the world has ever seen. Did you know that in addition to being a painter, sculptor and architect, he was also an accomplished engineer and inventor whose ideas were way ahead of their time?

He conceptualised many machines such as helicopters, automobiles, armoured vehicles, robots and calculators. In fact, many of his ideas were so futuristic that those machines couldn't even be built at that time!

Leonardo da Vinci drew thousands of precise and detailed technical drawings showing his ideas.

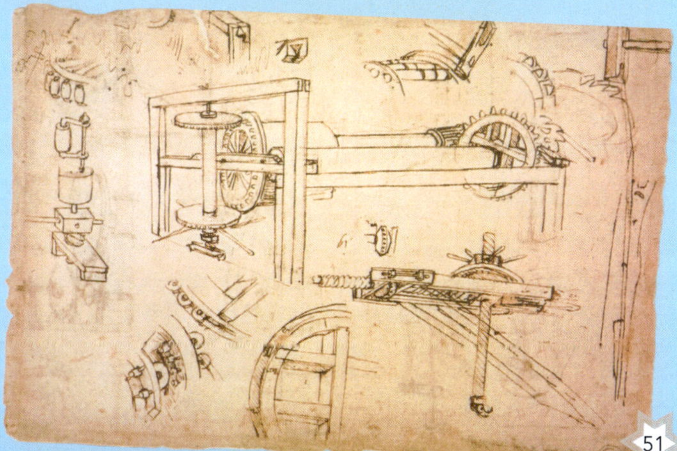

True or False?

Do you remember what you have learnt about engineering so far? Test yourself with this quiz!

Which sentences are true and which are false?

1. A civil engineer designs, develops and tests aircraft.
2. The Great Pyramid in Giza was made of 2.3 million blocks of stone.
3. It took 200 years to build the Great Wall of China.
4. Engineers do a lot of problem-solving at work.
5. Shinkansen trains were redesigned to mimic a hummingbird's beak.
6. Velcro fasteners were invented by a Swiss engineer.
7. James Blyth's house was the first in the world to have wind-powered electricity.
8. The International Space Station (ISS) is operated jointly by 15 space agencies.
9. Leonardo da Vinci built the world's first helicopter.
10. The air on Mars has less oxygen than the air on the Earth.

Find the answers on page 55!

Project Work

Let's use engineering to build a launcher with ice cream sticks!

What you need

- Six ice cream sticks
- Three rubber bands
- A plastic spoon
- A small piece of aluminium foil crushed into a ball

What you need to do

1. Stack five ice cream sticks and secure one end using a rubber band.

2. Slide the last ice cream stick between the bottom stick and the rest of the stack. Secure the other end with a rubber band.

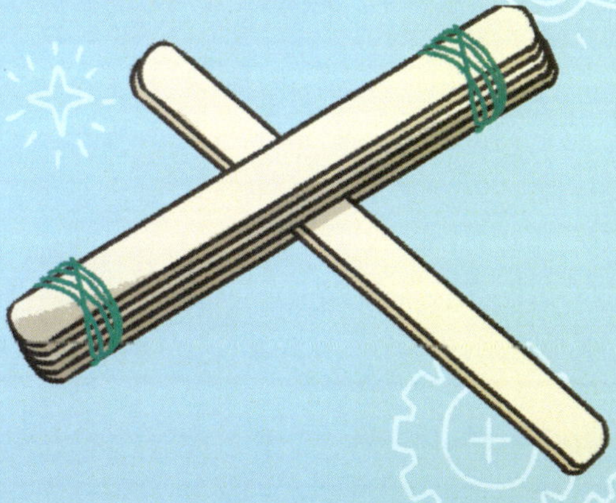

3. Place the plastic spoon on top of the single ice cream stick and secure it with a rubber band.

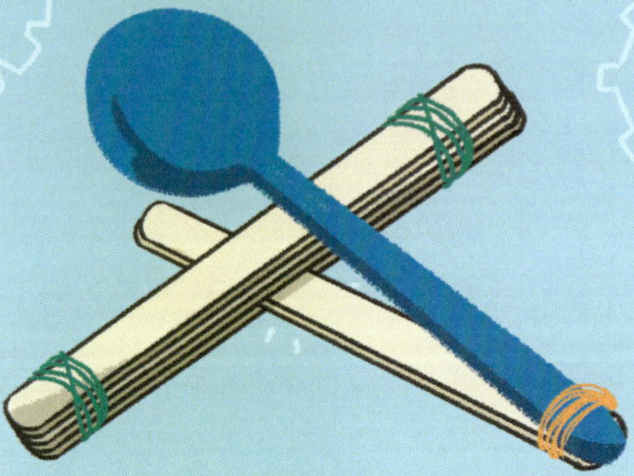

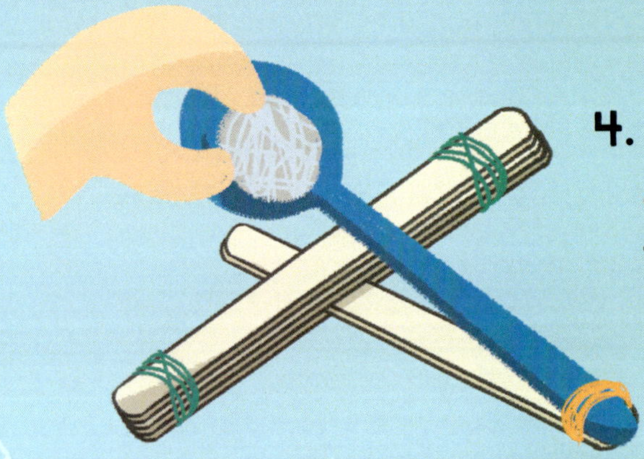

4. Place the ball of aluminium foil in the spoon.

5. Press the spoon down and release it to watch the ball fly!

Answers

Detective Work (page 30)

(a) Eiffel Tower (Paris, France)
(b) Sydney Opera House (Sydney, Australia)
(c) Big Ben (London, United Kingdom)
(d) Leaning tower of Pisa (Pisa, Italy)
(e) St. Basil's Cathedral (Moscow, Russia)
(f) Colosseum Rome (Rome, Italy)
(g) Marina Bay Sands (Singapore)
(h) Palm Jumeirah (Dubai, United Arab Emirates)

True or False? (page 52)

1. False
2. True
3. False
4. True
5. False
6. True
7. True
8. False
9. False
10. True

I'M A FUTURE SCIENTIST!

The *I'm a Future Scientist!* series of full-colour books for 6–12 year olds will spark sustained interest in scientific fields, such as botany, zoology, marine biology, conservation and the environment, astronomy, and many more, delivering primary-school-level Science learning points in an engaging and relatable way! Through clearly written educational articles, fun cartoons, suggested hands-on activities, as well as full-colour photographs and illustrations, these books are the perfect companions for budding scientists to delve further into a wide range of scientific fields.